CORNWALL
Land of Legend

JOY WILSON

GW00707466

BOSSINEY BOOKS

First published in 1989 by
Bossiney Books
St Teath, Bodmin, Cornwall.

Typeset and Printed by
Clowes Book Printers
St Columb, Cornwall.

Bound by R Booth (Bookbinders) Ltd
Mabe Burnthouse, Cornwall

All Rights Reserved
© 1989 Joy Wilson

PLATE ACKNOWLEDGMENTS
Front and back cover photography
by Ray Bishop

Ray Bishop: pages 87, 12, 16, 27, 28,
36, 38, 39, 41, 49, 50, 51, 52, 53, 56,
57, 63, 64, 69, 82, 84, 88, 93

Felicity Young: pages 3, 7, 18, 30, 33,
40, 62, 72

Cambridge University: page 44

Damon and Joy Wilson: pages 20, 21,
24, 46, 48, 55, 59, 60, 61, 66, 68, 71,
73, 74, 76, 78, 80, 83, 85, 90

William and Mary Photography: page 5

About the author
and the book

Joy Wilson was born and bred in Liverpool in pre-Beatle era. She was at school at Merchant Taylors' and then spent four years at Trinity College, Dublin, reading French and English Literature. A year in France teaching was followed by a few months in Leicester where she met Colin Wilson, her husband.

She worked as a Librarian in London and then a year after 'The Outsider' was published in 1956 they moved to Cornwall – for six months they thought – but they've been here ever since, making their home at Gorran.

In 1985 Joy contributed a chapter to 'Westcountry Mysteries', introduced by her husband Colin. In 1986 she made a major contribution to the Bossiney list 'Around St Austell Bay', the author's words accompanied by a wealth of old photographs and picture postcards. Then came 'East Cornwall in the Old Days' – she again skilfully combined text and old pictures.

Now comes 'Cornwall – Land of Legend'. Here she is on the trail of Tristan: the story of his fatal meeting with Iseult, the drama of their illicit love and the betrayal of the Cornish King Mark. It is a saga which has caught the imagination of people through the centuries.

Joy Wilson

4

Tristan and Iseult in Cornwall

by Joy Wilson

THERE are still many secrets to be unearthed in the Cornish countryside. This is a quest, made during the summertime, to look for the truth behind a Cornish legend known the world over.

Cornwall is an ancient land with many legends that have been handed down by word of mouth through the years by generations of Cornish people. Stories that continually change in constant retelling, embroidered by time but often based on true events.

Just one of the legends told in Cornwall became known in time as the world's greatest love-story. The story of Tristan's birth and later his fatal meeting with Iseult. The magic power of the love-potion taken in error, the drama of their illicit love and their betrayal of the Cornish king, Mark, has all caught the imagination of poets, minstrels and writers through the centuries, and has been retold in many different ways even up to the present day.

But the original setting of this story of the lovers was in Cornwall, and two of the main characters in it almost certainly really existed in the Cornwall of the sixth century. When I set out to investigate the evidence, still to be found today in the Cornish countryside, of that remote and distant time I felt tempted to believe that the events on which this dramatic legend was originally based might really once have happened here at the court of King Mark.

So it seemed to me an exciting challenge to follow up the clues to be found in the earliest version of the story known, which was first told in Cornwall and only later written down. With a camera and notebook, and on occasions accompanied by that accomplished

Part of the ancient kingdom where Tristan and Iseult's tragic drama took place.

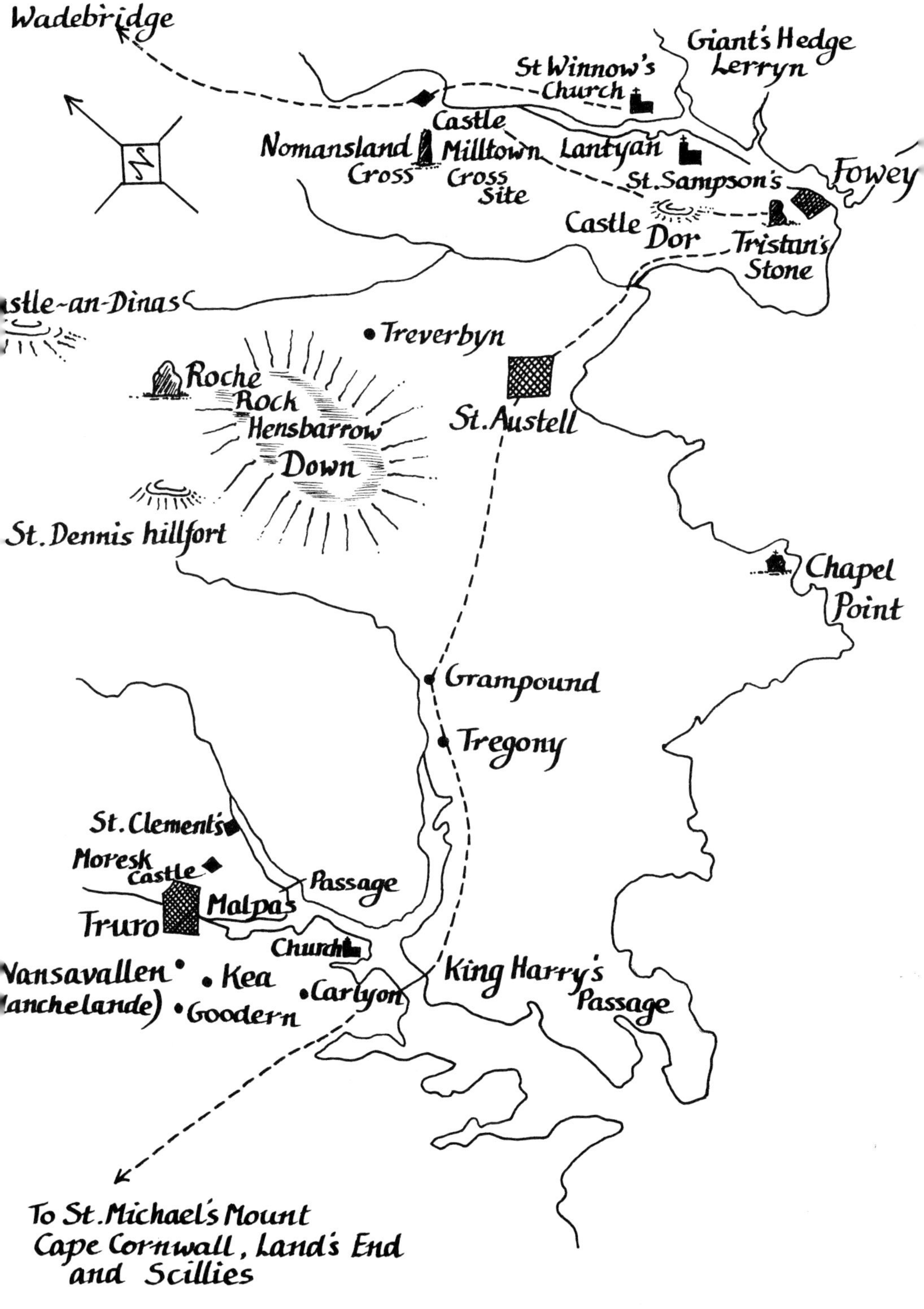

Wadebridge

Giant's Hedge
Lerryn

St Winnow's
Church

Castle

Nomansland
Cross

Milltown
Cross
Site

Lantyan

St. Sampson's

Fowey

Castle Dor

Tristan's
Stone

stle-an-Dinas

Treverbyn

St. Austell

Roche
Rock

Hensbarrow

Down

St. Dennis hillfort

Chapel
Point

Grampound

Tregony

St. Clement's

Moresk
Castle

Passage

Truro

Malpas

Church

Vansavallen
(anchelande)

Kea

Goodern

Carlyon

King Harry's
Passage

To St. Michael's Mount
Cape Cornwall, Land's End
and Scillies

Cornish photographer Ray Bishop, I set out to record the long shadow that this famous lovestory of Tristan and Iseult still casts on the Cornwall of today. On the way I was to encounter other legends of saints and sinners that were linked to theirs in time and detail.

The search led me into many byways. I hope that this account of it may attract others to explore some of the places that I found myself drawn to; parts of the county sometimes little frequented and away from the usual tourist tracks. But the real beginning was on the Fowey peninsula in south Cornwall at the foot of the Tristan Stone. There I tried to decipher the sixth century inscription that seems to prove that a Prince Tristan really had existed then, and also the puzzle of his relationship to the then King of Cornwall, Mark. Close by there was the earthwork fortress of Castle Dor to visit, and then later I crossed the Cornish moors and inland high ground over to the north coast, on the trail of the king which led me to the great promontory of Tintagel. There I was to come across exciting new evidence that has only recently emerged, of the truth about a sixth century royal presence at both these important Cornish sites.

In quiet contrast there was also a peaceful time to spend in the fields and ancient oakwoods of the valley of Lantyan, with close by the tidal inlets of the River Fowey, once the landing places from the sea, to explore.

Later I wandered farther afield along the switchback narrow lanes of St Kea parish, south-west of Truro, once the hunting territory of Blancheland described in the story. With the help of an old nineteenth century map I was able to follow in the footsteps of the lovers. Along the ancient tracks through Moresk that still lead down to the once important fording-place at Malpas Passage. Then I went to St Michael's Mount to look from the harbour with new eyes across to Marazion. It was there the market was held at which the hermit Ogrin obtained the fine silk for Iseult's dress that she wore to meet with the king once more.

From the jagged cliffs at Land's End, and climbing the less well-known but equally dramatic headland of Cape Cornwall in West

The 'great promontory of Tintagel', steeped in legend and bristling with layers of history.

Penwith, I looked out over the sea towards the Scilly Isles on the far horizon with their memories of Tristan's birthplace, Lyonesse, now long ago submerged beneath the waves.

My main guide through all these explorations was the poem that is the earliest version of the story of Tristan and Iseult that exists today. This poem was sung or recited for the first time here in Cornwall by an Anglo-Norman minstrel, Béroul, who came by sea from France in Richard Lionheart's time. He earned his bread by bringing news and entertainment from afar to the people in the isolated wooden castles of his feudal lord at Cardinham and Restormel in south Cornwall.

There, standing before the central fire in the Great Hall in front of the assembled company, the poet sang to the accompaniment of his harp with realist detail and humour too, of the dramatic and scandalous events that had taken place at the court of a Celtic king in the same part of Cornwall at an earlier time. It was a tale of love and adultery, magic and betrayal. Béroul had heard the bare bones of the story he told from the ordinary people he met as he journeyed across Cornwall. From them he heard an earthy tale of real human passions that had involved the family of one of their earlier Cornish rulers, including happenings colourful enough to be remembered and handed down through the generations.

In the poem that Béroul made from this story that so caught his imagination, he recorded the names that he had been told of the real characters involved and also gave many of the Cornish place-names for the areas through which the lovers travelled in their wanderings. Then he added clear vignettes of description of the Cornish country-side that are still recognisable today.

This is the bare nucleus of the story he told in which I found the clues embedded.

Looking across the wide expanse of Mount's Bay towards St Michael's Mount.

Cornwall – Land of Legend

TRISTAN was born a Celtic prince in the country of Lyonesse, now long ago submerged under the turbulent sea beyond Land's End. His mother, Blancheflower, was a sister of King Mark who ruled over a large part of the land of Cornwall in the sixth century of our history.

Now Blancheflower had eloped with the handsome Lord of Lyonesse against her royal brother's will. But unfortunately not long after their marriage her brave warrior husband was killed in battle. Overwhelmed by her loss Blancheflower herself died just after giving birth to their son.

The orphan child remained in Lyonesse in the care of a faithful retainer, Governal. He was christened Tristan which means sadness, because of his origin.

Time passed and the boy grew up well skilled as a hunter and warrior, renowned also for his playing of the harp and the songs he sang to its accompaniment. When he reached the early years of manhood he set out with Governal to seek experience and adventure in foreign lands.

After many wanderings Fate brought their ship close to the rocky shoreline of the lands ruled over by his uncle King Mark. Tristan and Governal landed in Cornwall and found their way to Mark's court which was then at the King's main summer stronghold situated on the great promontory of Tintagel. There Tristan was made welcome and his knightly skills admired, especially the music of his harp.

At this time King Mark's rule over this northern part of Cornwall

St Winnow on the banks of the River Fowey, once part of King Mark's domain.

12

was threatened by the annual arrival on the coast there of Prince Morholt, the brother of the Queen of Ireland. He was a ruthless man who demanded an annual tribute from the Cornish. Each year 300 young Cornish men and girls were taken back to Ireland as slaves, together with 300 pounds of silver and of tin.

Not one of the lords assembled at the court of Mark had courage enough to challenge Morholt in battle. When Tristan realised this he asked the King to knight him so that he could become the King's Champion himself. He had to reveal that he was the Prince of Lyonesse and also Mark's nephew and so equal in rank to Morholt, whom he challenged in single combat.

King Mark was overjoyed to find his nephew once more but feared greatly that he might lose him in the dangerous undertaking. However, Tristan was quite determined to fight and destroy the evil Morholt's power over the kingdom of Cornwall once and for all.

The combat took place on the Isle of St Samson a few days later. As the heavily armoured Prince Morholt tied up his boat on the sandy shore of the island Tristan also disembarked but allowed his own small craft to drift away with the current. Only one boat would be needed, he said, to carry back the victor after the fight to the death was ended.

There commenced a desperate struggle in which both men were wounded many times. At last with his remaining strength Tristan managed to strike off his enemy's plumed helmet and split open his head with his sword. A small triangular splinter from the edge of the sword blade broke off and lodged in the fatal wound. Felled to the ground, the dying Irish prince was carried to the boat and taken back to Ireland by his sorrowing followers. At the Irish court the splinter from Tristan's sword was extracted from the wound in the dead man's head by Morholt's sister the Irish queen.

In triumph the victorious Tristan returned to Tintagel, where the many serious wounds that he had received in the battle all healed save one. This was the result of a poisoned spear thrust into the flesh of his thigh made by the treacherous Morholt. The ugly wound festered and there seemed no cure. Its stench was such that everyone was driven away except his friend the faithful Governal. Finally, in despair, Tristan asked King Mark for a small boat without sail or oars so that he could embark from the beach and allow the waves and currents to carry him to a far distant place where he might perhaps find healing. The King at first tried hard to dissuade him but finally

Tristan slaying the 'giant snake-like dragon' with his magic sword.

ordered the boat to be prepared.

The vagaries of wind and tide carried Tristan's small craft on an erratic course which ended when it beached itself on a strand in Ireland. There the haunting music that he drew from his harp as he laid helpless in the boat finally attracted the notice of the Irish king.

Without knowing the identity of the wounded knight he ordered his daughter, the fair Iseult, who like her mother was skilled in healing arts, to send special herbs to heal Tristan's deadly wound. Such was their power that once more restored to health Tristan embarked for Cornwall without once seeing the Princess Iseult or revealing his identity.

King Mark was overjoyed by Tristan's unhoped for return from his mysterious voyage. He now resolved to make him his heir although many of the Cornish lords at his court showed bitter hostility to the idea. Instead they put pressure on the King to marry

15

with the idea of preventing Tristan from inheriting the kingdom. Mark was reluctant, and one day seeing in his garden two swallows fighting over a long shining red gold hair he picked it up saying that he would only consent to marriage with the woman from whose head it had come.

Because of his affection for his uncle Tristan set out to search for the lady. He wandered far and wide in vain until fate brought him once more back to Ireland. There he pretended to be a merchant called Tantris to disguise his links with the Cornish court. Now at this time the fertile green territories of the Irish king were being laid waste by a giant snake-like dragon and in desperation the king had promised his daughter Iseult's hand to its slayer.

Tristan tracked the malevolent beast to its lair, and after a great struggle he was able to kill it with his magic sword, cutting out its loathesome tongue as a trophy and proof of his deed. But as he wandered back on foot through the ravaged lands he became affected by the tongue's venom and fell to the ground in a deadly faint.

In the meantime the scheming seneschal of the Irish king claimed to have despatched the serpent himself and quickly asked for the princess's hand. But Princess Iseult did not like or believe him and set out herself to find the true victor. Out in the wastelands she found Tristan lying unconscious. She had him brought back to the palace and nursed him slowly back to health.

One day when Tristan was immersed naked in a wooden bath of water scented with herbs to heal his wounds, Iseult idly drew his sword from its scabbard. There on its blade she saw the triangular notch. She quickly retrieved the fragment of metal that had come from her uncle Morholt's head and found that it fitted exactly. With the sword clutched in her hand and blind with a desire for vengeance she ran at the helpless Tristan to take his life in exchange for her uncle's.

But Brangain, her maid and confidante, at once rushed to restrain her with the warning that if Tristan died Iseult would have to marry the lying steward. Reluctantly Iseult forgave Tristan. By producing the severed tongue of the serpent he was later able to convince the

The magic love potion which brought such passion and sorrow to the two lovers Tristan and Iseult.

king that he was the true slayer of the beast and in return was offered Iseult's hand in marriage. Tristan accepted, but realising that the golden hair that had been the swallows' prize had come from Iseult's head, he claimed her on his uncle's behalf.

True to his word the Irish king agreed, but the queen was anxious that her daughter should not have a loveless marriage with an unknown man, and prepared, using all her arts, a magic love-potion. She intended it to be drunk by King Mark and her daughter on their wedding night, and its mysterious and irresistible power would last three years exactly.

On the sea voyage home, escorting the princess Iseult accompanied by Brangain back to King Mark, Tristan became thirsty from the flying salt spray and singing to the music of his harp. He asked for wine to quench his thirst. In her haste the maid Brangain accidentally poured into a single golden goblet the love-potion that had been prepared for the wedding night. Unknowing, Tristan shared with Iseult the drink in the goblet. Immediately, its magic power took effect and from that moment on they only had eyes for each other. The few isolated days that they spent together as the small craft sped over the Irish sea waves finally sealed their love.

At long last the boat reached the Cornish shore and tied up below Port Hern, the Irongate, the landing place at the foot of Tintagel rock. A strange episode was to take place on King Mark's wedding night. Iseult arranged that Brangain, who was a virgin, should secretly take her place under cover of darkness in King Mark's bed, lest he should discover her own infidelity. The ruse worked and Iseult then quietly assumed her place at King Mark's side. The king fell deeply in love with his beautiful Irish bride and was grateful to his nephew Tristan for bringing her to him.

As the summer progressed, Mark's court moved to Lantyan, his castle on a hill near the banks of a great river in the south part of Cornwall. While the king rode out over his lands hunting deer and boar through thick forest glades Tristan and Iseult were often able to meet secretly and make love together in the king's chamber. But some of the lords at court had become more envious of Tristan than ever. Gradually they became aware of the illicit liaison between him and Queen Iseult and were quick to inform the king. On one fatal day Mark discovered the two lovers together and exiled his nephew from the court to live in a neighbouring town.

But Tristan and Iseult continued to meet in secret. It chanced that

Tintagel's Port Hern, the Irongate, where Tristan and Iseult's boat finally tied up after the long voyage from Ireland.

at Lantyan a clear stream flowed down from a spring in a nearby orchard and passed beneath the window of the chamber. Tristan would break off the brittle twigs from an ancient apple tree and cast them into the stream. The clear water tumbling around the stones carried the twigs in a line formed by the current to where Iseult could see them as they floated past her window. Then she would secretly hasten to the orchard for an assignation among the safe shadows of the apple tree branches.

Like many Celtic knights, Mark kept at his court for his amusement, a dwarf, in this case an evil sorcerer called Frocin. Guided by his black magic skills the dwarf was able to betray the lovers' rendezvous to his royal master.

So one night, the unhappy Mark went into the orchard and concealed himself on a branch of a great oak that overhung the stream, intending to eavesdrop as the lovers met below on the mossy bank. As Tristan approached moonlight glinted on the surface of the water revealing a reflection of the king's dark shadow on the branch

Castle by Lantyan overlooking the Fowey River where King Mark held court.

above. Iseult, approaching, also saw its outline but neither of the lovers made any sign. Aware of the king's presence Iseult fiercely reproached Tristan for summoning her from her chamber at so late an hour . . . while in his reply Tristan claimed that he had come there only to beg her to intercede with the king on his behalf as a loving nephew. Iseult's quick response was that her love for Tristan was indeed merely a natural filial regard for her husband's nephew.

The lovers then parted leaving King Mark in his hiding place convinced of their innocence. He turned his anger against the scheming dwarf who temporarily fled the court telling his dark secrets to an old bent thorntree on his way.

So Tristan was reinstated at court once more with all his privileges. He slept in the king's chamber on the floor on a pallet, as was the custom in those days for favoured retainers.

One night at midnight the king rose and went off with the dwarf who had used his evil powers to get back into favour. Frocin had made a trap for the lovers by scattering white flour on the floor between the beds. When the king departed Tristan sprang from his pallet to the queen's bed in one leap leaving no footprint. But the exertion opened up a half-healed hunting wound on his thigh so that heavy drops of blood stained the queen's sheet. Tristan lovingly clasped Iseult in a close embrace, but then hearing the king's abrupt return with the treacherous dwarf he made a desperate leap back to his own pallet. A trail of drops of blood stained the flour on the floor while in the shadowy doorway the dwarf Frocin gleefully held up a lamp to reveal the lovers' guilt to the king.

This time King Mark was unable to forgive. In a violent passion he condemned the two lovers to death. Tristan's sentence was that he should be burned on a huge brushwood pyre already being built on a distant hill. Mark's soldiers dragged him quickly away under heavy guard.

On the route to the hill Tristan and his guards passed a small lonely chapel built from the stones of the beach out on a rocky

Apple orchards still flourished at Golant when this old picture postcard was taken.

21

promontory by the southern sea. There a hermit kept a light burning to warn mariners of the many jagged rocks concealed at high tide. Tristan pleaded with his captors to allow him to enter the little chapel to make a last confession and to pray for his soul. Since the chapel had only one narrow door they allowed him to enter. But in the wall high above the stone altar was a tiny square window filled with rare red glass. Below it outside the fragmented slatey cliff formed a precipice above the restless sea.

Tristan made a sudden bid for freedom. He leapt on the altar and forced the window open, squeezing his body through the gap he leapt down to a small sloping platform halfway down the cliff. It broke his fall and he was able to scramble sideways down to the beach below. There Governal, who had secretly followed behind the guards with their prisoner was able to catch Tristan up on to his horse as he fled across the sand. He had brought with him Tristan's sword and gave it to him as they galloped away from the frustrated pursuers. Ever since that day said the story teller, Béroul, the site of the ancient chapel has been known to the Cornish people as Le Saut Tristan – Tristan's Leap.

Now at first Iseult was condemned also by King Mark to the flames of the pyre but the great lord Dinas of Dinan, the king's seneschal, and a true friend to the lovers, pleaded successfully for her life. However in his jealous rage Mark decided on a sordid humiliation of his erring queen. The unwilling and terrified Iseult was handed over by him to the uncouth leader of a band of 100 unsightly lepers. They were all filthy, dressed in tattered grey rags and supported by rough wooden crutches, sounding their doleful clappers to warn people out of their path. Iseult was roughly led away by them towards their group of isolated hovels some distance from the palace near a lonely crossroads.

By chance, as they were dragging her through reeds flanking a treacherous marsh the leper band passed the spot where Tristan was hiding in a thicket with his rescuer. Quickly seizing the opportunity while the lepers were off guard struggling over the wet ground Tristan rescued the unhappy Iseult from her tormentors.

Then the two lovers accompanied by the faithful Governal fled away together to hide deep in the great and mysterious Forest of Moresk, which covered a large central area of King Mark's domains. Ordinary people feared to enter this forest and seldom ventured past the thorn trees on its fringe. The two lovers began a fugitive and

Looking towards St Clement on the banks of the Tresillian river where once the giant forest of Moresk covered the land.

nomadic life in its shelter.

They were kept alive by Tristan's skill as an archer. He had a bow of laburnum wood which never failed to send the arrow to its mark. The lovers lived on venison and nuts from the wildwood but had no milk or salt or bread. Their only shelter was a bower that they constructed of cut branches with a couch of leaves. Enduring hardship they remained in the forest growing thin but still obsessed with their fated love for each other.

One day their wanderings led them out of the forest to a distant hermitage built on a lonely granite outcrop overlooking a wild moor. Ogrin the hermit warned them that King Mark had placed a reward of 100 silver marks on Tristan's head. In his piety the holy man urged Tristan to make a confession and repent of his illicit passion. But when Iseult told Ogrin of the love-potion and its irresistible effect he took pity on the pair and allowed them to shelter for one night in the hermitage. Next day for safety the lovers returned once more to their bleak forest existence.

Time passed, and one day when Tristan had been out hunting

with his dog Husdant since sunrise, the heat of the hot midday sun beating down on his head caused him to return to their shelter. He stripped to his linen underbritches and lay down to rest beside Iseult who wore only her long chemise. His friend Governal was far afield hunting so that the lovers were alone. By chance a solitary forester passed their grotto, and recognising the pair, rushed off to repeat his discovery at the court at Lantyan, a full day's ride away.

The woodman's agitated arrival in hope of reward, was witnessed by King Mark who ordered him to wait at the foot of the Croiz Rouge, a stone cross painted with red ochre marking the boundary near the palace. It stood at a fork in the road where the dead were often buried. There Mark eventually joined him, alone, and the forester led him across country to the lovers' retreat. Stooping low under the boughs as he entered, Mark drew his sword. He saw the lovers lying asleep side by side while between them unsheathed was placed the bright sword of Tristan, separating the two. Suddenly the king felt uncertain of their guilt and hesitated. He was touched by Iseult's frail beauty and seeing that her wedding ring set with emeralds was loose on her thin hand he replaced it with the ring that she had given him. He removed Tristan's sword and replaced it with his own. Through the leafy canopy overhead a sunbeam flickered over Iseult's closed eyes burning the delicate skin of her cheek. Mark laid one of his riding gloves across the gap in the branches to shade her from the fierce rays. Then abruptly dismissing his forester guide he rode back to Lantyan.

When the two lovers woke at dusk they were in sad disarray. Iseult recognised Mark's ring and leather glove and Tristan the alien sword.

Until this time the strength of the love-potion had kept the pair aware only of each other and reckless of the privations of their outlaw existence. But a day or two soon afterwards the three years of the potion's fatal power expired. Tristan and Iseult were suddenly overwhelmed by the realisation of the sacrifices they had made to be together, and their treachery to King Mark. They travelled once more to the hermitage on the high rock and asked the hermit to write for them a letter asking the king's forgiveness. It was to be carried by Tristan to Lantyan and Mark was requested to leave his reply tied to the Croiz Rouge. Tristan's letter explained that he had sought and found Iseult for the king in the first place, and that when he had later found her helpless in the hands of the lepers he had had no choice but

Looking across the causeway towards St Michael's Mount from Marazion where Ogrin obtained a dress of royal purple for Iseult.

to rescue her and take her to seek refuge in the Forest of Moresk.

Tristan put himself in great peril taking the letter to Lantyan, where he called the king to the window and thrust it into his hand. In due course Mark's reply was hung on to the Croiz Rouge. He stated that he would take back Iseult as his queen once more, and that in three days time she must meet him at the Gue Aventuros, that is, the ford where things happen, otherwise known as the Mal Pas. Tristan was bidden to leave the country of Cornwall altogether.

Though the lovers still loved each other deeply, the blind obsession that had bewitched them until now was gone. Quietly they prepared for their parting. Iseult kept their hunting dog Husdant and gave to Tristan as a lovetoken a green jasper ring. If ever in the future he should need her he was to send the ring and Iseult would come to him at once, neither tower or fortress would keep her away.

Now in the meantime Ogrin the hermit had left his windswept hermitage on the high rock and journeyed to St Michael's Mount on Iseult's behalf. There at the market that was held weekly on the sandy shore he acquired for her by barter a dress of royal purple made of rare Baghdad silk, white and gray furs and a gentle nag all harnessed in gold. Thus instead of her drab forest rags Iseult would be regally dressed for the reunion with King Mark at the Mal Pas ford.

25

On a 'gentle nag' Iseult was led back to her husband, King Mark.

When the day came the rich colour of her clothes emphasised the beauty of Iseult's shining red gold hair and her sparkling green eyes. Sadly Tristan took the bridle of her little horse and, leading her across the narrow meadow that sloped down to the Perilous Ford, he solemnly handed her over to the king once more. He offered to prove his own honour by knightly combat but the envious knights of the court counselled Mark not to allow him to stay any longer at all.

Proudly Tristan said farewell and rode off in the direction of the distant coast. Iseult followed him sadly with her eyes until he was lost to view. Then once more ceremoniously reinstated as Queen she rode back with Mark to Lantyan.

From there, the next day, she led a grand procession down the paved road to the chapel of St Sampson at the monastery built by the saint under the shoulder of the hill overlooking the wide river below.

Malpas Passage with the site of Moresk Castle in the trees on the skyline.

In the chapel Iseult made a thank offering of a rich embroidered and jewelled robe. It was shown ever after that time on all the feast days of the saints.

That night at the palace at Lantyan the festivities for her return lasted until the moon had waned.

Now instead of departing across the sea to Britanny as ordered, Tristan had gone into hiding once more. His refuge was a wooden storage cellar under the house of a humble forester named Orri. There he secretly stayed to receive news of the court and of Iseult's relations with Mark.

It was fortunate that he did so as some of the unfriendly lords again caused trouble. This time they demanded that Iseult should clear herself of all guilt by undergoing a public Trial by Ordeal. Black with fury at the lords' enmity King Mark came to Iseult's side. On seeing him she half fainted fearing that Tristan's whereabouts had been discovered, until Mark told her of the demand for a trial.

Quick to make a bargain, Iseult said that she would be willing to submit to a trial if it was staged at Blancheland, a part of Mark's realm where he had his hunting grounds on the high heathland. She requested that King Arthur and his knights should be present as witnesses.

When Mark agreed to this, Iseult contrived to send a secret message to Tristan asking him to come on the day of the trial to the Mal Pas, the ford that led across the river to Blancheland. He was to disguise himself as a leper to avoid recognition by King Mark and his court and to station himself on a rocky mound near the marshy ground where planks were laid across the treacherous mud of the river.

When the day of the trial came Tristan was there on the mound dressed in the patched grey rags of a leper with a begging bowl and wooden clapper to warn the crowds to keep clear. From each person who pushed past him he demanded alms, even from King Arthur and King Mark themselves. Three of the hostile lords came by and demanded directions from the despised leper. Following the way indicated they wandered sideways into the marsh, sinking and struggling until only tufts of hair were visible.

But when most of the company had safely negotiated the perils of

Tristan, in the grimy disguise of a leper, safely carried his love across the perilous ford.

28

the Mal Pas Iseult herself rode down to the ford. She was dressed in a fine robe of silk with a long cloak trimmed with ermine trailing on the ground. Her red gold hair was braided with ribbons into two long plaits and a gold circlet rested on her brow. The motley crowd pressed around her curious to see how she would make the miry passage over to Blancheland dressed in such finery.

Iseult expertly dismounted and looped her stirrups over the saddle, then, giving her small mount a sharp slap on the rump she sent it trotting delicately across the dark muddy surface to the other side. Near her Tristan in his grimy disguise leaned heavily on his crooked rough hewn crutch. Iseult approached him and boldly demanded that he should carry her across the treacherous ford on his hunchback shoulders. He feigned incomprehension until Iseult ordered him to stoop and clambered up on to his back urging him across the ford. Tristan lurched unsteadily through the mud once or twice pretending to stumble. When they reached the foot of the path on the Blancheland side he demanded alms from Iseult as she slid down from his back. But she ignored him and rode her little palfrey up the steep woodland track towards the open heath beyond and the king's hunting lodge.

The next day Iseult had to prove her innocence. In the high meadow tents were pitched and the two kings sat in state as witnesses. In front of them on a piece of fine silk cloth were spread out all the holy Christian reliquaries from the chapels of Cornwall; ivory caskets, bejewelled and painted, containing the fragmented bones of saints.

Placing her right hand on the most important reliquary of all Iseult swore a solemn oath before the assembled company. She said that no man had ever come between her thighs save only King Mark, her lawful husband – and the poor leper who had carried her on his back over the dangerous Mal Pas ford.

This impressive but ambiguous statement was accepted in good faith by all the people present and Iseult's innocence was deemed proven.

The great King Arthur and his retinue returned once more to his capital of Caerleon in Wales and King Mark and his queen rode back to the castle at Lantyan. Tristan remained in hiding, but this time he was given refuge in the great castle of Dinas in Penwith, by Dinan, his friend among the powerful Cornish lords at Mark's court.

On the surface it seemed that Mark and Iseult were reconciled at last. But as time went on informers disclosed to the king that whenever he was away at his hunting lodge in pursuit of the deer of Blancheland, Tristan was still secretly meeting Iseult. The two evilly disposed lords at the court planned to spy on the lovers through the small window of the king's chamber. They hid in a clump of yellow irises on the banks of the stream outside and with a knife bound on to a long stick drew aside the thin curtain hoping to see into the interior.

Just as Tristan entered the room Iseult turning towards him, perceived the outline of a man's head through the fine linen of the curtain. Quickly she made a sign to Tristan to put an arrow into his laburnum bow. Looking up he saw the shadowy outline and took aim. The swift arrow pierced the man's eye and he fell dead into the stream while his associate fled away in terror. In this way the last of the enemies of the lovers was dispersed but Iseult realised that their troubles were still not over. This time she begged Tristan to leave her and to live far away for his own safety as Mark would never forgive him.

Tristan realised at last the truth of this. For the safety of them both he had to go. Sadly he took leave of Iseult and with his friend Governal boarded a ship in the river that took them across the Channel to Brittany to find refuge.

There, so the Breton legends about Mark and Tristan say, Tristan lived in a royal residence where six roads meet at Carhaix. He passed several years in loneliness, until at last he met a Breton princess also with the name of Iseult; Iseult of the White Hands. Attracted by her rare name and despairing of ever seeing his Cornish Iseult again he took her as his wife. The two lived together in harmony but because of Tristan's fateful love for the first Iseult, their marriage was never consummated. In time Tristan was drawn away on many adventures and took part in many battles.

Eventually he received a very bad wound and in spite of his wife's nursing there seemed little hope of recovery. In despair Tristan asked for the jasper ring to be sent to Cornwall with a message to Iseult the Fair begging her to come and cure him once more with her healing arts. He ordered that if the returning ship had Iseult on board it was to carry a pure white sail, but if she had refused to come to him then the sail was to be entirely black.

When she received this message the abiding strength of her love for Tristan led Iseult to forsake her husband Mark and the court. She immediately left Lantyan and set sail for Brittany.

Meanwhile Tristan was struggling on the edge of life. His wife, Iseult of the White Hands tenderly took care of him, but hearing of his first love's approach she gave way to natural jealousy. When the ship appeared on the horizon she reported to him wrongly that it carried a jet black sail.

As the ship beached on the strand, thinking that his true love had in the end failed him, Tristan gave up the struggle to live. As Iseult the Fair walked up the hill into the town she heard all the bells solemnly tolling to mark his passing. With the news that her lover Tristan was dead, Iseult's heart finally broke. She lay down on the pallet beside his lifeless body and died in his arms.

Eventually King Mark arrived in Brittany to seek his wife. He heard at last the full story of the magic love-potion and the fate of the two lovers. Generous of heart and full of sadness Mark at last understood and was able to forgive the two beings that he had loved most in the world.

Arrangements were made by him for the ship to carry the two bodies back to Cornwall. There the two lovers were buried side by side with honour and regret.

From the two graves two plants sprang, the wild hazel and the yellow honeysuckle, forever intertwined, as they grow still in the hedges of Cornwall.

Iseult the Fair sailed to Brittany to heal her lover but his wife, Iseult of the White Hands, was none too pleased.

The Tristan Stone

The Tristan Stone stands lonely and enigmatic by the side of the road that leads to Fowey town and harbour. Only when the afternoon sunlight slanted obliquely across the stone's granite surface could I make out the small rounded lettering of the sixth century inscription carved in two vertical columns and very difficult to decipher in its weathered condition. In the Latin of the time it reads:

DRUSTANUS HIC IACIT / / CUNOMORI FILIUS
Here lies Tristan, the son of Cunomorus

Apparently D easily became T in Cornish and so Drustanus is in fact the same as Tristan, while Cunomorus, or Cynwawr refers to Marcus Cunomorus, King Mark of Cornwall. Tristan was therefore in reality his son.

So through the ages this ancient memorial stone has borne silent witness to the real existence of two of the chief characters of the love story. If Tristan was truly the son of King Mark perhaps it was the earthy drama of his incestuous love relationship with his father's wife that was remembered and retold many times by the Cornish people. Then a long time afterwards it was heard by the poet who changed the relationship into the more respectable one of uncle and nephew.

Originally the stone stood close to the great earthwork of Castle Dor in a small enclosure by the ancient road that was probably the family cemetery. The stone has been moved many times and I found a 1785 map of Lescrow farm nearby that shows the stone lying in a field and describes it as being at least ten feet high, three feet taller than today. In Tudor times, John Leland, an intrepid traveller in Cornwall, gave its measurements as being a foot taller than that and wider as well. Intriguingly he also described the existence of a third vertical line of inscription on the stone which read:

34

CUM DOMINA CLUSILLA
with the Lady Clusilla

Now Clusilla is an Irish name and could be transposed into the rare Cornish name of Eselt. Both have the meaning of golden meadow flower and could refer to the golden-haired princess Iseult of Béroul's story.

But the damage that it suffered through the years has caused the great stone to weather and split. If the third line of inscription existed it would be called the Tristan and Iseult Stone and would provide evidence of the one time existence of all the main characters of the love story. Since it has gone some scholars doubt that the third line was ever there. However, looking closely at the stone I could see that from the right side a large piece has broken off and the third line might well have been inscribed there once.

Still clearly to be seen on the reverse side of the stone but less often noticed is a sixth century T shaped cross carved in relief. King Mark is known to have been a new convert to Christianity who encouraged St Sampson to pause in his saintly vagabondage and found a small monastery at Golant on the King's lands overlooking the River Fowey. Now the T shaped cross was also a powerful image used by the pagan Druids who regarded it as the symbol of eternity and often cut sacred trees to the shape of a T. St Sampson had studied Druid wisdom in his youth in Wales so perhaps this ancient Christian symbol of the Tristan stone betrays also a slight echo of recently supplanted pagan beliefs in Mark's kingdom. Certainly in later times someone thought it necessary to add a carved cross in a circle high up on the side of the stone perhaps to sanctify it a little more.

Time and change have not been able to erode the stone's basic message: that once it marked the grave of Prince Tristan, the son of King Mark of Cornwall.

Overleaf, the massive Tristan Stone.

King Mark of Cornwall

In the story of Tristan and Iseult King Mark has an unenviable role to play, as a victim of betrayal and jealousy. But in real life he is well documented as a powerful ruler of sixth century Cornwall. His name is included in a Dark Age list of the High Kings of Dumnonia who ruled in the Westcountry. There he appears under the title of Cynwawr or in Latin Cunomorus, meaning 'horse' a sacred creature in Celtic mythology and so a fit name for a king.

When much of Europe was locked in conflict during the turbulent times of the sixth century, King Mark is recorded as maintaining a rule of peace and prosperity in Cornwall. He was an early convert to

Kilmarth and the possible site of the king's burial mound.

Polkerris harbour, part of the ancient Celtic living site of Kilmarth.

Celtic Christianity when many of the people on the upland moors still lived in pagan superstition under the sway of the Druids.

Confirmation of his reign and that his main stronghold was in South Cornwall on the Fowey peninsula is given in the life of Saint Paul de Leon, written by a Breton monk. He said that while the saint was in Cornwall: 'his fame reached the ears of King Marc, who is also known by the name of Cunomor, a powerful monarch under whose rule lived people of four different languages – probably Welsh, Irish, Cornish and Breton. This King desiring to settle firmly and in enduring fashion the foundations of the Christian faith which had only lately been laid in that country and to unite all his subjects in obedience to it . . . Paul came to the place which in their language is called Caer Bannhed, where now the bones of the same king rest . . .'

Now it seems that Caer Bannhed which means 'the high place of the red deer' may well have been the original name of the great earthwork fortress of Castle Dor which stands on a hill overlooking the river Fowey in South Cornwall. Through the ages this windswept place has been associated with King Mark as the site of his palace. It was this impressive site with the spacious enclosure within its curved earthen banks that first gave me the idea of tracing the Tristan legend in the Cornish countryside. So it was not altogether a welcome discovery to find that archaeologists are having second thoughts about linking King Mark with Castle Dor at all.

But nearby, in the shelter of the valley below, is the old farmhouse of Lantyan and this is the name of the place which Béroul the poet gave to King Mark's southern citadel, perhaps following what he had been told by the local people of his time. Not far away from here, only a mile or so to the west, is another trace of Mark's links with this area. Overlooking the wide sweep of St Austell bay is the ancient Celtic living site of Kilmarth, which means Mark's Retreat or resting-place. There below the old house among its sheltering trees in a pasture that slopes towards the cliff edge, is a mysterious mound that is said by some to be the grave of King Mark. Certainly from this lonely spot

The royal palace at Lantyan.

there is an impressive view over what would once have been the king's territories, from the distant moorland of inland Cornwall to the coast and the restless waves of the bay below with the jagged cliffs around Polkerris and beyond. It seems a fit site for a King's burial place.

On the eastern bank of the River Fowey climbing up a hill above the ancient post of Lerryn, I found another possible link showing King Mark's rule over this part of Cornwall.

From the inlet at Lerryn across fields and woodland to the West Looe river at least eight miles away, runs a formidable earth and stone barrier crowned with trees. It is still in places over eight feet high with its steepest and most impregnable side facing north. Although the date of its construction is not known – some people attributed it to the work of the Devil – it is much more likely to have been constructed under the orders of King Mark to defend his territories bordering the Fowey estuary from Irish incursions. It has been thought that the Giant's Hedge may once have continued across the Fowey, over the hill past Castle Dor to the shore of the bay below Kilmarth. There is no trace left of it there today.

It seems that the stormy episode in Cornish history, when the Irish made repeated incursions into Cornwall, was quite forgotten until recently when evidence of Irish placenames and carved symbols in stone were discovered here. But long ago Béroul had recorded in his poem the sad history of Irish aggression and demands for tin tribute and slaves that led to Tristan's great fight to the death with the evil Irish Lord Morholt. In this way true history was preserved in the legend.

The farmhouse at Lantyan.

41

Castle Dor

The high earthen banks of the Iron Age hill fort Castle Dor, near Fowey, I have been told, once protected the great wooden palace or feasting hall of King Mark when the stronghold was re-used in the turbulent times of the sixth century.

The pre-war excavation carried out inside the earthwork seemed to confirm this view when an impressive pattern of square postholes was discovered. They indicated that two great halls, a kitchen, granaries and a porter's hut had once stood within the shelter of the high banks. A paved entrance, unusual for the time, was also uncovered while blue and yellow glass beads and two beautifully moulded fragments of a woman's bangles in green and ultramarine glass were also found. Although they were dated as pre-Roman these trinkets seemed to confirm a tenuous link with the romantic Iseult story.

However, recently, a new archaeological analysis of these finds has completely changed this picture. Apparently insufficient evidence has been found to prove that Castle Dor was ever used as the residence of a sixth century Cornish king or of his subjects. That elaborate layout of 'palace' postholes has now been interpreted as only a small complex of humble wooden huts of an Iron Age settlement. The extra postholes belonged to the stout porches built onto the small huts to keep out the Cornish weather.

Perhaps another excavation might change this view for it is known that many other hill forts in south Cornwall were re-used extensively in the sixth century. To me it seemed strange that Castle Dor, the largest and most impressive of all, was not. Perhaps centuries of deep ploughing of the rich soil in the enclosure have destroyed the evidence.

The impressive circular earthworks of Castle Dor.

However, even within the shelter of these great earthen banks Castle Dor would have been a draughty place to locate the king's palace. Westerly winds seem to blow there throughout the year and the ancient ridgeway which the fort was built to dominate passes uncomfortably close by. Through many centuries it was the chief route from North Cornwall to the southern harbours and like all tracks in Mark's time it would have been frequented by a turbulent and sometimes hostile stream of travellers, vagabonds and deserters.

So did the King simply garrison his soldiers and horses up here within its windy shelter to stand guard over the road and keep a watch over the river below? Perhaps as the poet's story tells, Mark's citadel was built closer to the river on a gentler wooded hill slope in the valley of Lantyan.

Tintagel

On the great black slate promontory of Tintagel, originally called Pendhu, which dominates that part of the North Cornwall coastline, it is said once stood the legendary fortress of the Cornish king. That was in the time long before the Normans came and the twelfth century castle was built there. Tintagel features improbably in the stories of the Arthurian cycle as the great King's legendary birthplace. But it is much more likely to have been King Mark's northern stronghold in his conflict with the Irish, just as recounted in the Tristan story.

Not long ago there seemed little proof of this at Tintagel itself. On visits all that I found were the labelled sites of a small Celtic monastery on the cliff edge, a medieval walled garden and chapel and the crumbling walls of the twelfth century castle clinging to the precipitous cliffs, the drama of its position capturing the imagination of every visitor.

But now in the last few years new evidence has been discovered that alters our picture of this historic site altogether. When a disastrous fire in the summer of 1983 destroyed fragile plant cover on the western side of the high plateau above the castle site, the damaging flames revealed the stone foundations of over 100 small sixth century buildings whose existence was quite unsuspected before. This complex of small stone outlines in the burnt turf, and possibly more impressive, the discovery of the foundations, as yet undated, of a hall over 80 feet long, on the highest part of the plateau overlooking the sea, make it likely that an important sixth century royal citadel was once sited here. It would have 'belonged in turn to the kings of the area if not of the whole of Cornwall.' In fact as one of the high kings of Dumnonia Mark would have ruled here.

On the mainland opposite stands Tintagel church, isolated near

A group of keen amateur archaeologists take a close look at some of the recently revealed evidence of past civilisation at Tintagel.

the cliff edge and surrounded by its lan or Celtic burial enclosure. But close to it, and much older than the present church, are several impressive grass covered mounds thought to be the Celtic Christian burial places of once important Dark Age people and rulers. Clearly visible from the promontory, perhaps these important graves were the focus of summer rituals held at the Tintagel citadel to reinforce King Mark's ancestral right to rule over his Cornish territories and people.

If you explore the paths on the promontory your feet are quite likely to uncover a broken red earthenware fragment from the soil. Many such fragments have been found here; all that remains of large cargoes of amphorae, containers of oil and wine and other luxuries imported here in the sixth century from the eastern Mediterranean and North Africa. They were unloaded at the landing place of Port Hern, the Irongate, and carried up the steep paths to the plateau above. Full amphorae weighing 80 lbs apiece would have been difficult to carry.

King Mark was one of the powerful Cornish rulers who retained

The mystifying burial mound in Tintagel churchyard.

the loyalty of the local lords by distributing occasional rich imports of oil and wine. They were paid for by bartering hides and the tin streamed from the moors that he had received in tribute from his subjects.

So Tristan would have come to Mark's court first in summertime, when it was assembled at Tintagel in the better weather for the royal ceremonies and the occasional landing of rich cargoes in the haven below. From the rocky platform below the Irongate Tristan would have been carried to his boat for the hazardous voyage in search of healing that brought him to Ireland and the fateful meeting with Iseult the Irish princess.

But as Béroul's story makes clear, and he had probably been told, King Mark's chief feasting hall and palace was not Tintagel but in a more sheltered setting at Lantyan. There close to the River Fowey he could control his southern Cornish territories and the sea route to Brittany as well.

Lantyan

Two separate narrow high-banked lanes lead down from the Fowey road on the ridge into the valley that lies below Castle Dor. Each a hazard for motorists, they both drop steeply to the farmplace of Lantyan. Once the lords of the manor of Lantyan had jurisdiction over many other manors and land scattered throughout Cornwall from St Germans to the Lizard. Were they the last vestiges of the territories of the royal demesne over which King Mark's rule once held sway?

Today at Lantyan the three-storied stone farmhouse, at right-angles to the road, looks out benignly over a secluded garden where the rhododendrons planted at the beginning of this century have become tall trees. A path across the lawn led me to a remarkable stone sundial of strange and unique design, that tells the hours but nothing

Castle – the manor house today.

'A path across the lawn led to a remarkable stone sundial'.

The author in a doorway of one of the old farm buildings marked on the ordnance survey map as 'remains of ancient manor house'.

of its history or how it came to be in the garden.

One of the old farm buildings that are tucked under the shelter of the hill is marked on the ordnance survey map as 'remains of ancient manor house'. Could this have once been part of the ancient palace of King Mark? Certainly the great stones used in its construction and the arrow slits in the walls make it seem very old. But the King's great hall was probably built of wood and this valley site is too low lying and vulnerable to attack for a sixth century stronghold.

Behind the farmhouse runs the Saint's Way by which Saint Sampson and other Celtic saints from Wales and Ireland crossed the Cornish peninsula. Only a little way along, where it skirts the edge of Lantyan Wood and climbs to the top of the hill, I followed it on foot to find the large field which has been called Mark's Gate for as long as can be remembered. From here an ancient track leads through the dense oakwoods that have hardly changed from the wildwood down to the edge of Woodgate Pill, a tidal inlet that was once the Fowey River landing place for Lantyan and Castle Dor. From Mark's Gate

Woodgate Pill, a tidal inlet that was once the Fowey River landing place for Lantyan and Castle Dor.

through Lantyan Wood I found another way that leads down to the ancient crossing place over the river to St Winnow on the eastern bank. On the hillside behind this Celtic church site there was once a deer park, so these two old tracks from Mark's Gate could once have given access to the King's eastern territories and hunting grounds. From the oakwood shelter of Woodgate Pill Tristan could have sailed downriver and across the southern sea to exile in Brittany.

Reversing my steps I followed the Saint's Way a mile or so inland, passing the hamlet at Milltown to reach the old manor house of Castle sheltered among rare trees.

Several clues seem to point to this place at the head of the Lantyan valley as the most likely site for King Mark's southern palace where many of the events in the love story took place. Castle or Kestle in Cornish means a hill top stronghold. Behind the present manor house stands Great Hill and exploring on the heights I found a gentle south-facing slope with a strategic view over the Fowey river where it curves past St Winnow towards its estuary. Just below this spot there was once a paved ford across to the eastern bank, and to the west, across the Lantyan valley, it is possible to see distant Castle Dor and the ridgeway running along the skyline. Looking upstream an alert sentry here could have seen as far as the site of Restormel Castle where an earlier wooden stronghold would have stood, and beyond to the high ground of Bodmin Moor on the distant horizon.

This place was known as Chastell in 1340 but on the earliest documents it was Lantyan Parva, part of the great Lantyan desmesne. An old map that gives the field names seems to tell a significant story. There is Castle Meadow, Castle Moor, Hunting Down, and Orchard down by the stream. Rather more sinister is the field, close to a turn in the road, that is called Gallows Down.

Today at the foot of the hill four ancient high-banked roads meet at the bridge over the stream, perhaps an indication that, although remote today, Castle was once a place of importance. The early Georgian manor house is close by with pointed Gothic windows fashionable at that time. A spring flows strongly into a fern-shrouded trough set in the herb garden wall and the house is known to stand on a site where many earlier ones were built in the past. Past the formal

Mark's Gate from the Saints path.

Castle, where 'four ancient crossroads meet at the bridge'.

garden at the side of the house I followed a track that joins up with another one coming up from the river. Both end abruptly and inexplicably half way up Great Hill. Maybe once they had continued to the site of King Mark's citadel on the hill's southern flank. Only excavation here could provide any proof.

Certainly the sunlit site, the ancient name of Lantyan, the distant hunting grounds and the orchard close to the stream are just as described in the story. Hazel and honeysuckle, the symbols of the lovers flourish in the hedges of Lantyan, intertwined in riotous growth. Perhaps Béroul the minstrel came here once.

Tregaminion Cross – Croiz Rouge

On the boundary of Castle by Lantyan this cross once stood. So it seems possible that it was the Croiz Rouge of Beroul's story on which the messages between Tristan and King Mark were hung. Red ochre was often applied to crosses and signposts to make them stand out and this would account for the colour of the cross in the story.

This cross has had a chequered history. At the time of the Black Death a troop of wandering flagellant monks paused beside it and to atone for the people's sins, thought to have caused the plague, they scourged themselves into a frenzy. A long time later the cross was uprooted and used as a footbridge over a stream. Then it was rediscovered and sold for £5 and taken to Devon. Only a fortnight later it was claimed back by the Rashleigh family who set it up in an octagonal base of unknown origin with a strange zigzag and dot design. They placed it in Tregaminion Churchyard not far from Kilmarth on the Fowey peninsula. There I found it half hidden by giant rhododendrons with the damage suffered from the feet that once passed over it clearly to be seen.

Tregaminnion Cross, overleaf, possibly the ancient Croiz Rouge.

St Sampson's Isle and Tristan's Battle with the Morholt

Below the site at Castle by Lantyan in the middle of the river Fowey and just before it passes St Winnow church there was once an Isle St Sampson. It was mentioned in a document of 1301. Brother Robert of Pelyn, perhaps a humble successor to St Sampson himself, lived here in solitude and the island could well have been the site of Tristan's epic battle with the Irish prince. But time changes the bed of a river like everything else and nowadays at low tide there are only

Fowey River where 'there was once an Isle of St Sampson'.

St Helen's oratory above Porthleddon Beach.

shifting sandbanks to be seen at this spot.

The other traditional site for this fight has always been the Isle of Samson in Scilly. There Tristan's struggle to the death with the Morholt was believed to have taken place on the sandy flats that lie between the two haunted peaks of the island. The stone walls of a very early Celtic hermit's cell were found here buried in the sand and some think that St Sampson may have left his monastery at Golant for Lenten meditation here.

Tristan would have embarked for the Isles of Scilly from Porthleddon beach, the broad harbour. Watched over by the ruins of St Helen's oratory and sheltered by the protective bulk of Cape Cornwall this little beach near St Just in Penwith, although stony and inhospitable today, was once the main departure point for direct passage by sea to Scilly.

At the beginning of this century its fine sand surface was dressed for the tin that had been carried on to it from the mining valley of Kenidjack close by. Then the lighter sand on the beach was washed away out to sea leaving it useless as a harbour and it has never returned.

The twin hills of Samson, Isles of Scilly.

The Band of Lepers

There was a leper at Lantyan according to Béroul's story. He was the leader of a band of comrades 100 strong, and to him, in jealousy, King Mark handed over poor Iseult to be dragged away to their grimy refuge. Later in the story, at Iseult's suggestion Tristan adopts the disguise of a leper for the important encounter at Malpas Ford.

An unlikely scourge today, in early times leprosy was rife in Cornwall, brought here by sea-traders from the East. So probably there were lepers at Lantyan in King Mark's time. Only a mile or two away from there, not far from No Man's Land crossroads on the Lostwithiel road there was a lazar house called Maudlin set in a

Kiggon, near Truro, site of another lazar house in early times.

No Man's Land crossroads where there was a lazar house.

remote field. There lepers lived in sad isolation dependent on alms. Legally declared dead to the world they were dressed in rough homespun with a stick to support diseased limbs. They carried a bell to give warning and a wooden cup for alms. Small humanity was shown to them and there was little medical help. No wonder they were often depicted as repellent and of uncertain temper.

On the edge of a reedy marsh near the Tresillian river not far from Malpas another Cornish lazar house was situated in early times. It stood at Kiggon, near Truro and from there a leper could easily have taken the river path that leads by St Clement to Malpas Ford, so Tristan's strange choice of disguise becomes more credible. Perhaps Béroul the poet knew the area well and was aware of the leper colony there.

Orchards in Lantyan

In these early times when much of this part of Cornwall was forested, harbouring wild boar and an occasional wolf pack, and the rest was wild heathland or open moor, then the walled enclosure of an orchard with short grass underfoot and the shade of apple hung branches, provided a perfect trysting place for lovers, safe from the harsh world outside.

For a long time there was a large orchard at Castle, not far from where the stables are today. The stream flows nearby and trees

An apple orchard was the perfect trysting place for lovers.

Apple orchards at Lantyan.

King Mark concealed himself on a branch above a stream to eavesdrop on his wife and her lover.

overhang it, just as in the story when King Mark in jealousy concealed himself on a branch above the water to eavesdrop on Tristan and Iseult, and their clandestine meeting in the shelter of the apple trees.

Not so long ago the river Fowey was renowned for the many orchards along its banks or on farms nearby. The apples were grown for food or cider, often given in lieu of wages. The hillsides sloping towards the river allowed any frosty air to drain away to the valley below and so were ideal for growing apples.

It seems that the land of Cornwall was associated with apples a very long time ago. In a Greek play written by Euripides in the fifth century BC, there is a verse that speaks of an earthly paradise, almost certainly Cornwall:

> *To the strand of the daughters of the sunset,*
> *The apple trees, the singing and the gold ...*
> *HIPPOLYTUS*

62

St Sampson at Golant

The church of Saint Sampson looks out over the sandy tidal reaches of the River Fowey, standing on the hill above the village and harbour of Golant. It was to the church of St Sampson that, legend tells, Iseult rode in a procession with coloured flags flying, along a paved road from Lantyan. She brought as a thank-offering for her reconciliation with King Mark the rich gift of an embroidered robe in silver and gold. It became a treasure of the church for centuries to come.

But in Iseult's time all that would have been here would have been St Sampson's little round hut and those of his few monks. They would probably have been built of reed and cob, grouped round the

St Sampson at Golant.

holy well still here today beside the church porch. Sampson's small chapel of wattle or local wood probably occupied a small area where the present chancel stands. Enclosed within the oval earthen bank, this would be the extent of the little Celtic monastery founded here by the saint. His cousin, who wrote his 'Life' describes how Sampson paused at Golant on a journey of holy vagabondage across Cornwall, while awaiting a sea passage over to Brittany. At the invitation of the local ruler here, probably King Mark, he founded this monastery to help convert the people to Christian beliefs.

Perhaps appropriately, only on Sunday is it permitted to walk along the railway track here to locate the cave that was once St Sampson's refuge beside the river. Holy men in Celtic times liked to immerse themselves in freezing water as an aid to penance, prayer and meditation, and so Sampson chose this cave close to the river.

Under a thick curtain of creeper I found it hard to locate in the fractured rock of the hillside. Inside, exactly as it is described in St Sampson's 'Life' water drips continually and uncomfortably from the roof and splashes down on the big stones fallen to the pebble covered floor. The cave is very deep and narrow and goes a long way back into the hill. It was not hard to believe the story that Sampson was forced to vanquish a fierce serpent-like dragon that lived in the cave's depths. When he entered the cave it was disturbed and afraid. It bit wildly at its own tail in rage only to find itself ensnared around its scaly neck with a tight noose made from the Saint's white woven girdle. Sampson then threw it down from a great height to the river and told it to live no longer. Only then was Golant and the wide district around rid of the serpent's evil miasma. The cave was then sanctified and became the saint's spartan retreat.

The cave that gave refuge to St Sampson. A serpent-like dragon lived here in the Saint's day but now it is filled with a different kind of menace – twentieth century rubbish!

The Hermitage of Roche Rock

When, through privation, Tristan and Iseult eventually wandered away from their woodland refuge in search of nourishment, they came at last to the edge of the forest. As the trees gradually thinned out they continued on, and crossed over a wild and lonely tract of heathland before coming by chance upon the solitary hermitage of Ogrin the holy man. Twice the lovers returned to seek forgiveness and his prayers for their well being, and in time Tristan was able to make use of Ogrin's skill in letter writing, rare at that time, to communicate with the estranged King Mark at Lantyan.

The Forest of Moresk used then to extend far into the hinterland and from its borders the erratic wanderings of the two lovers, on the wild moorland that extended beyond it, might well have brought them at last to the foot of Roche Rock. It is known that in very early times there was a hermitage here upon the summit, perhaps the first in Cornwall.

Roche Rock is a solitary outcrop on the edge of the high downs that lie between Bodmin and St Austell town. The gaunt and tumbled mass of black granite rises abruptly out of the surrounding moorland, and the sight of its high jagged outline in dark silhouette against the western horizon can arouse a feeling of awe in those that pass on the roads nearby. Local people living here used to think that the earth that once clothed its exposed granite sides had all been swept away by Noah's Flood, leaving the fractured rockface forever stark and denuded, a windswept perch for passing witches and malevolent demons.

Perhaps this place was once the setting for pagan rites. When

The hermitage perched on top of Roche Rock.

Christianity was first brought to Cornwall by Celtic saints from Wales and Ireland, between the two highest pinnacles of Roche Rock, a small oratory was built in a space hollowed out of the rock face, with rough walls constructed from random stones gathered up from where they lay in the bracken below. Water came from a small never-failing spring among the boulders, and in this draughty shelter there lived a long succession of dedicated holy men whose solitary prayers helped to sanctify this place. Ogrin the hermit may well have been one of their number.

Long after the time of Tristan and Mark, at the end of the Middle Ages, a more elaborate hermitage was built here with walls of quarried ashlar stone strong enough to withstand the winds of centuries. The chapel with an east-facing window was constructed on top of the original rock-hewn hermit's cell that had always been reached by a precarious wooden ladder. It was dedicated to the Archangel Michael, long known as the saint of high places and the vanquisher of evil forces.

A Thursday market was held on the strand at Marazion opposite St Michael's Mount.

The market at St Michael's Mount

Ogrin the hermit would have had to make a long journey on foot over wild country to reach the market at St Michael's Mount, there to obtain by 'cash, credit or barter' fine clothes of silk and ermine for Iseult to wear for the reconciliation with her husband, King Mark.

Marazion (Marghas-byghan) means 'little market' in Cornish, and a 'Thursday market' was held here as well in this village on the sandy strand opposite St Michael's Mount during a time span of hundreds of years. Today searchers walk across these sands at low tide looking for the rare pebbles of agate, topaz and amethyst that are sometimes to be found. It is hard to imagine the busy markets that once took place here when Cornish ingots of tin, hides and wool were bartered for luxury goods brought from afar, by sea-traders from the eastern Mediterranean and France.

So Ogrin might perhaps have found silk for sale, brought here after a long and arduous journey from the East, but the cloth would have been extremely expensive because of its rarity. During the sixth century a few silkworm eggs were stolen and illegally smuggled out of China, to be brought to the merchants of Byzantium. Once the great Chinese secret of silk-making was learnt by them, this city and the city of Baghdad held on to the monopoly for 500 years. Silk was so rare in western lands that the cloth made from it was reserved for royalty alone to wear. The fine dress made for Iseult of deep purple silk and ermine would have been a truly royal garment, when at this time the best clothes available for even the most prosperous in Cornwall were simply made of fine linen or wool.

All the goods exchanged by barter at the markets of Marazion would have been landed or shipped out from the harbour in the shelter of the Mount, whose history as a port may go back to prehistoric times.

Tristan's leap and escape from his captors

On the way by which they went
A chapel on a hill
Was built on a rocky pinnacle
It overlooked the sea in the north-east wind.
The part called a chancel was built on a mound
Beyond was nothing but the cliff
The hill is smooth slatey rock
If a squirrel jumped from there
It would be killed I guarantee . . .

BÉROUL, THE ROMANCE OF TRISTAN

Tristan made the most of his chances and escaped from his captors near here.

Chapel Point, close to Mevagissey harbour, possibly the spot where Tristan leapt to freedom.

This seems to be an almost exact description of Chapel Point, a long sea-girt promontory quite close to the harbour of Mevagissey on the opposite shore of St Austell Bay to the Fowey peninsula and Lantyan.

Perhaps the minstrel Béroul saw this place on his voyage from France, for he must have landed somewhere on this stretch of Cornish coast. Certainly he stated in his poem that 'from time immemorial the country people have called this place Tristan's Leap.'

It might have been this well known story of Tristan's escape and its association with Chapel Point that inspired Sir Henry de Bodrugan to make a similar escape from near this spot a few centuries later. Lawless and piratical, Bodrugan owned all the land here and lived in a fortified manor house at the head of the valley nearby. When his fortunes finally waned and the tide of kingly politics turned against him, he made a daring escape from his enemies by jumping his horse down the cliff here to reach a waiting ship that carried him to safety and exile overseas.

From Colona beach on the west side of Chapel Point, if you look up towards the summit of the promontory, a small level platform is visible beneath the trees in the garden of the middle house built there. Forming part of a rockery a few courses of foundation walls remain. They are all that remains of an ancient 'Lighthouse' chapel that stood here in medieval times on the exposed rock summit of the promontory. In this lonely place a hermit tended a flickering light that shone out seawards through the narrow chapel window. For centuries it was a warning to seafarers of the dangerous submerged rocks off the end of the point and provided a beacon guide to the safer havens beyond in the shelter of the bay.

From Gallows Down and the execution pyre ordered by King Mark at Castle-by-Lantyan to Chapel Point with its beach and ancient chapel would be quite a distance by land, but not so far by sea. Standing here on the empty beach in spring when the sand is strewn with flotsam and piles of seaweed cast up by the waves, it is not so hard to picture Tristan's daring leap down the slatey precipitous cliff and the horseback escape from his enemies across the sand.

The Forest of Moresk –
a day's ride from Lantyan

The southern route through Cornwall from Plymouth and upcountry, crosses the narrow bridge over the Tresillian river where the last skirmish of the Civil War took place. Then after passing through Tresillian village, leaving the tidal mudflats of the river behind, the road climbs a long winding hill before its gentle descent into the city of Truro.

On each side of the busy road in scattered patches venerable oak trees can be seen growing. They are all that is left of the original woodland that once clothed all the hillsides and valleys here. Today

The broad mud flats left when the tide goes out at Tresillian, deep in the heartland of Moresk Forest.

Looking from the site of Moresk Castle towards Malpas and Blancheland.

the crooked branches of these old hardwood trees only half conceal the serried ranks of a modern conifer plantation. The old trees are the last remnants of the great Forest of Moresk which once covered all this part of Cornwall.

Oak, ash and hazel have probably grown here since the days of the prehistoric wildwood, and through the years the trees have provided fuel and charcoal for men; timber for their homes and ships, oak bark for tanning, and acorns to feed the pigs. Within the forest glades deer used to roam. This made the forest a privileged hunting ground in the royal possession of the early Cornish kings, probably including King Mark himself.

For those who did not fear to enter it, the forest provided a rough shelter, and here Tristan and Iseult are said to have sought refuge. From the trees they cut leafy oak boughs and used them to construct a bower well concealed in the remotest depths of the forest; a place of safety to hide after their desperate flight from Lantyan and King Mark's jealous rage.

Where the main road finally leaves Tresillian village I found a little metal gate half lost in the hedge. It opened onto the unsignposted footpath that follows the ups and downs of the Tresillian river bank all the way to Malpas Passage. Even on a warm July day when I walked this path, between hedges with honeysuckle and wild roses in full flower, it was quite deserted. It starts by skirting the edge of the reedy marsh close to where the lepers of medieval times once lived in the isolation of their humble huts at Kiggon. There a few years ago in the corner of a wooden shed a strangely carved stone head was found that had come from the lazar chapel here.

After continuing around Pencalenick Point the path climbs slightly uphill and I followed it in the shade of the branches of the ancient oaks of the Forest of Moresk. They clothe the banks of the river here as their ancestors had always done. They seem to grow as thickly here today as they must have done when the clerks of the Domesday Book came to calculate the area of this great forest and its value.

Past the small river landing place with its boats below the ancient church of St Clement, the path continues on around the foot of Dinas Hill. Near the clump of trees on its summit is the site where Moresk Castle once stood before its final destruction by order of an English king. There must have been an earlier Celtic fortification here, perhaps a wooden watchtower which would have commanded the extensive and strategic view up river and eastward over the royal territories towards Lantyan. Downstream towards Malpas Passage a watch could have been kept on the ancient ford with its dangerous crossing over the Truro river to Blancheland on the southern bank.

The remnants of the great Moresk Forest.

Malpas – the ford
where things happen

The ford where things happen, the Mal Pas of Béroul's story can be found in Cornwall today. Just south of Truro in tiered rows on the hill the houses and cottages of the small village of Malpas look out towards the place where, between heavily wooded banks on the Kea parish – Blancheland – and Roseland sides, the Tresillian creek and the Truro river meet. They merge later with the waters of the Fal.

In Malpas today several old paths still approach the little waterfront which must once have been the ancient fording place to cross the river. Here the old road that follows the river bank from Truro meets the footpath that I followed from Tresillian. It leads past the village of St Clement and Moresk and from the top of the hill above Malpas village, an ancient track, not much used now, still leads down towards the water. All these routes must have been used by early travellers to reach this important river crossing place.

Nowadays in summer the steamers from Falmouth, at high tide in summer, moor at the landing stage and there is still an occasional foot ferry over to the Roseland bank. Small boats bob at anchor in the current all the year. But when the tide in the river ebbs and only a ribbon of water is left, a dramatic change takes place. Extensive shining mudflats are revealed, strewn with bladderwrack and tidal debris, a haunt of sea birds and waders, but the gleaming surface of the mud seems quite impassible for heavier beings.

Mal Pas means 'bad place', or 'treacherous ford', but recently an experimental crossing on foot over the mudflats was made, from below the ferry cottage on the Roseland bank over to the Malpas landing place. Several people completed this trip, muddy and triumphant, but careful tidal calculation and protective clothing were needed, certainly not a safe undertaking for everyday.

The real Mal Pas, the hazardous ford of the story over which

The village of Malpas looking towards Blancheland.

Iseult in her fine clothes was carried on Tristan's back in his leper disguise, is described as a series of narrow planks laid on the mud to reach to the Blancheland shore. Straying from the right place, three of the unfriendly lords were engulfed by the mud. Certainly at this place today such a crossing on foot would be quite impossible. Perhaps in those earlier times the Truro river was shallower and the mud flats less extensive and treacherous, but the crossing to Blancheland must have been always a Mal Pas, a dangerous ford, just as it is described in the story of the lovers' adventures.

Blancheland

Opposite the village of Malpas on the far river bank, the oak trees grow close together and their sturdy branches lean down to the water. An ancient hollow way, worn deep in the rock, leaves the shore and climbs steeply uphill through the trees. At its foot there is an immense boulder on the edge of the mud on which Tristan might have stood to say farewell when Iseult had leapt down from his back after fording the river. She would have urged her small horse up this same trackway through the woods on her journey to King Mark's hunting lodge in Blancheland, where the scene of her Ordeal by holy relics was to take place.

This area south west of Truro above the river is St Kea parish today. It includes a wide stretch of territory with fertile lands close to the river and scrub and heath on the uplands beyond. Blancheland is not a name that is found on any modern map but in the heart of Kea parish an avenue of trees leads towards an old farm called 'Chyrwin' built on the site of an original Celtic homestead, just where the rich pastureland begins to give way to the heath of the higher ground. The ground here is widely scattered with fragments of white quartz and Chygwin, or Alba Landa on old documents means White land, the Blancheland that was once the royal hunting ground.

The track that Iseult followed from the river leads to a lane that passes close to the narrow ruined tower of Old Kea church. It stands in trees above the tidal inlet where St Kea first moored his boat after his voyage to Cornwall from Glastonbury. Poor St Kea fell foul of the local ruler Teudar, a predecessor of King Mark, when he sheltered a frightened stag fleeing from the royal hunting party. In a wild rage King Teudar knocked out one of the Saint's teeth so that by

Old Kea Church.

Carlyon, an old farmhouse in Blancheland or St Kea parish as it is now.

association in later time the holy well of St Kea became a favourite resort for toothache cures. Teudar repented his fit of bad temper and encouraged the Saint to found a small Celtic monastery on this spot, well endowed with the fertile lands around.

On her way to the hunting grounds Iseult would have seen here, not the pinnacles of the lonely church tower but instead, the oak shingled roof of the Saint's oratory and the beehive huts of his monks. Her route would have taken her past other places whose names have

A hollow way still leads from the landing place at Blancheland.

Goodern, an impressive rectangular earthwork.

an Arthurian ring, Carlyon and Nancavallan, today a farm in the valley below the Truro-Falmouth road whose name means Vale of Apples, perhaps a reminder of Avalon.

Once up on the high ground, heath, rough pasture and today old mineworkings stretch along the horizon as far as Chacewater, which means the hunting ground near water, surely a clear memory that this part of Blancheland was once the great hunting territory of the Cornish kings.

Not far away in the corner of a large level meadow with a commanding view over the surrounding country I found an impressive rectangular earthwork, its enclosing earthen banks defined by the twisted thorn trees that grow upon them. This is Goodern and old documents speak of this place as having been once a 'castle' of irascible King Teudar who here fought a battle against Christians. During the battle he was killed by a fall from his horse, and is thought to have been buried beneath a large tree-crowned barrow that stands close by. Teudar's Christian successor King Mark is thought to have used Goodern as a hunting lodge. And in the level

The photograph shows a reliquary with a card reading:

THE RELIQUARY OF
S. PETROC
of Painted Ivory
Siculo-Arabic. Mid-12ᵗʰ Century
The work of Arab Craftsmen in Sicily
under the Norman Kings

It was on a reliquary such as this that Iseult had to swear her innocence.

meadow alongside perhaps the tournament and Iseult's Ordeal witnessed by the kings was staged.

An odd footnote is provided by a historian who tells how, in Tudor times, a local farmer here dug up at Goodern – within the enclosure – enough gold and silver to transform him from peasant to gentleman.

Tredruston and Hryt Eselt

A lonely signpost at a crossroads near Wadebridge in North Cornwall points the way down a narrow wire fenced road which leads to Tredruston. A Cornish Celt named Druston or Tristan once built his homestead on this sheltered valley hillside below St Breock Down. The modern signpost provides a silent proof that Druston/Tristan was a personal name used in very early times in Cornwall although almost unknown elsewhere. Perhaps this humble Celtic farmer was named after a prince of the time, the drama of whose illicit love story had become part of Cornish folklore.

At least 100 years before the poet Béroul came to Cornwall and heard this story, the people who lived on the wild Lizard peninsula knew all about the Princess Iseult's adventures at the Dangerous Ford. In a Charter of 976 AD a land boundary near St Keverne is defined. It included a remote crossing place over the little Porthallow river which had the name of Hryt Eselt, the Cornish for Iseult's Ford. This is the only record of this woman's name then quite unknown, until much later when the story of the lovers, first heard in Cornwall, captured the imagination of poets in half the countries of Europe.

If you explore the lattice work of lanes between Goonhilly Down and St Keverne, Eselt's Ford can still be found. A lane of medieval narrowness, once a packhorse trail, runs steeply downhill and crosses the little river flowing down the valley below Lesneague farm. From a perilous perch on the riverbank I photographed the large granite slabs of the original clapper bridge, now quite concealed under the present tarmac road surface. In its time it must have replaced the slippery stepping-stones of Hryt Eselt, the little ford here in Celtic times.

Pendinas, perched above Porthmeor beach at St Ives.

Pendinas St Ives

Dinan, the Cornish lord who was Tristan's friend at King Mark's court, is known to have owned the fortified stronghold on this headland, the 'Island' whose bulk still protects the fishermen's and artists' cottages of Downalong St Ives today. Pendinas fort was 'built on the peninsula and stony rok where now the town of St Ives stondeth', and it defended the sandy landing place below.

Dinan refused to ally himself with the jealous Cornish lords and gave help and secret shelter to Tristan when he was sent into solitary exile from King Mark's court. His friendly nature is confirmed by the help that he also gave to the Christian Irish princess St Ia, who, it is

87

said, after making a hazardous voyage from Ireland on an outsize leaf, landed on Porthmeor beach below his stronghold. In truth St Ia's 'leaf' was probably a greased hide and wicker coracle, an unfamiliar craft to Cornish eyes. St Ia persuaded the Lord Dinan to build her an oratory close to the sea where the parish church stands today. Her holy well is still to be found near Porthmeor beach where her first baptisms were made.

Other Irish missionaries had already arrived in this area and when Ia joined them her influence spread. But her ultimate fate was sad, ambushed and martyred by the pagan king Teudar, whose fiery nature became enraged by the Christian incursions into his territories. But Dinan and the other Lords in Penwith gave the saints a kinder welcome and ultimately they ensured that their holy bones and relics were preserved and their memories revered.

Brittany – Tristan's exile

In Brittany, I found that many legends exist about a certain King Marc'h, sometimes known as Conorre or Conomor, who died about 555 AD. Could there be a link with the Marcus Conomorus of the inscription on the Tristan Stone at Fowey?

The Breton King Marc'h certainly also experienced matrimonial problems. He had five wives in succession and his solution for matrimonial discord was to cut each of their throats in turn. Murderous tendencies also emerged in his efforts to kill St Sampson, who by this time had left Golant and the shores of Cornwall to found his great monastery at Dol near Mont Saint Michel. Poisoned wine, a wild horse and a starving lion all failed to dispatch this holy man, and for his efforts King Marc'h was laid under a solemn curse.

Now the king's Breton citadel was at Carhaix in Finistère, on a lofty hill overlooking the place where many routes meet. It was to this citadel at Carhaix, Breton legends say, that Tristan came to live in his sad exile from Cornwall and his love. Here in time he married another Iseult, gentle Iseult of the White Hands.

'A ship with a white sail' carved on an old bench end in St Winnow Church.

The southernmost peninsula in Finistère is called PenMarc'h, named after the king, and close to it passed the ancient tin traders' sea-route from Cornwall. At PenMarc'h, as in Cornwall, a tempestuous sea once engulfed part of the land here and from a boat it is possible to see ancient dolmens and standing stones submerged below the waves.

When Tristan received his fatal wound, the Bretons say that it was to the sea's edge, among the rocks on the extreme tip of PenMarc'h, that he was carried to await the arrival of Iseult by sea bringing him healing once more. With the false report of a sombre black sail seen on the distant horizon, Tristan finally lost hope that she would come to him and died here in sorrow. Iseult landed on the shore too late and there is an ancient chapel here that marks the spot where the two lovers were eventually reunited in death.

King Mark of Cornwall, with his stronghold in Lantyan and his command over the estuary of the Fowey River, might well have maintained sovereignty over Finistère in Brittany. But in these legends the character of the Breton King Marc'h does seem to have suffered a sea-change for the worse.

Lyonesse seems only just out on the horizon on this old picture postcard of Cape Cornwall.

90

Tristan's Land of Lyonesse

Stories of a lost land persist in West Cornwall where the ancient name for Land's End was Pedn an Laaz. It meant 'end of the earth'. But in spite of this folk memories still remain of a beautiful and fertile land called Lyonesse that once existed beyond Land's End and Cape Cornwall, extending as far as the Isles of Scilly and southward towards Mount's Bay. A land that lies submerged today below the white crested Atlantic waves that roll in towards the jagged mainland coast.

All the versions of the love story state that Prince Tristan was born in Lyonesse and that this land was his by inheritance, many centuries before the fatal cataclysm that is said to have overwhelmed it.

On an old seventeenth century map printed in Holland I found some evidence that Tristan's land of Lyonesse could have been a living reality. The Seven Stones on which the Wolf Lighthouse stands today, above the waves beyond Land's End, are marked on this map as 'The Gulfe' with a Latin inscription which reads 'A land which sank having previously been exposed above the sea'. The Seven Stones are thought to be the tip of an extinct volcano and the Sennen fishermen used to speak of the city called Tregva or Lyons that once stood in its shelter and told tales of doors and windows that they had dredged up from this area in their nets.

Very much earlier, in the Anglo-Saxon Chronicle, a monk from Worcester confidently wrote that all the land here was totally destroyed on 11 November 1099. On that night, by the light of new moon, often a time of storm in Cornwall, a surge of tempestuous sea 'overflowed the shore and destroyed many persons and innumerable oxen and sheep.'

Now in Mount's Bay, near Penzance, when the sea recedes further than usual at stormy times of the year, witnesses have seen and even photographed the blackened and spongy remains of large treestumps with their root systems still embedded in the sand. Robert Hunt the folklorist who collected so many Cornish legends and stories in the nineteenth century from the people of Penwith, left a true account of how, as a schoolboy in Penzance, he and some friends had walked far out over the wet sands at extreme low tide. There they found tree trunks with fragments of leaves and beech nuts still preserved around them in the sand. In this way he confirmed the account given in the Anglo-Saxon Chronicle that the great inundation which destroyed a beech forest here, must have happened after a great autumn storm when the trees were still in leaf and bearing nuts.

Earlier than this schoolboy escapade, near Newlyn at Gwavas Point in 1835, a former lakebed was exposed in similar conditions. Surrounding it were the traces of marshy ground and trees. But most mysterious of all a dug-out canoe was found with an ancient coin embedded under the remains of a mast. This primitive craft must have floated on a shallow freshwater lake, separated by marsh and woodland from the open sea.

Until now this scattered evidence of a sunken land off Cornwall has been taken lightly or even quite discounted. But recent archaeo-logical discoveries on the Isles of Scilly do confirm that a dramatic submergence of land did take place there when a destructive ocean surge occurred, perhaps caused by an earthquake, in medieval times. On some of the islands including Samson, primitive man-made stone walls lead away from the land and continue on under the sea. Submerged burial cists and remains of huts have also been found, washed over by the sea today. All are evidence of a submerged central fertile plain that once joined all the islands into one.

Certainly earthquakes are not unknown in Cornwall. In 1757 one occurred which was centred on Penzance and shock waves extended throughout West Penwith and the surrounding seabed. Perhaps a similar cataclysm of even greater power could have brought about the tremendous tidal inundation that destroyed Tristan's hereditary kingdom for ever.

St Piran's flag streams bravely in the wind at Land's End, where, if legend is to be believed, the lost land of Lyonesse would have been clearly visible.

Epilogue

When the news of the tragic fate of Tristan and Iseult, through a cruel misunderstanding, was brought to King Mark, he set sail at once for Brittany to bring back their bodies to Cornwall across the southern sea. The story tells how in his sorrow, and because of the generosity of his forgiving nature, the King finally agreed for the two lovers to be buried side by side in Lantyan.

In time two bushes of hazel and honeysuckle sprang miraculously from the graves and grew strongly with branches, leaves and flowers forever intertwined.

Because in its history it has been moved so many times, it seems impossible now to know for certain whether the great Tristan Stone, that stands today near Fowey, could originally have been placed as a memorial stone above the spot where the lovers were buried. But the worn inscription on it remains as a silent witness to the historic existence of Tristan and Mark and their links with this part of Cornwall. In summertime on the earth and stone hedges of Blancheland and Lantyan I found hazel and honeysuckle still growing thickly. They seem to flourish there now just as they must have done when Béroul the poet came here so long ago and heard from the local people their story of the lovers at an earlier Cornish King's court. In the poet's retelling the closely entwined branches became a symbol of their doomed but lasting love.

Acknowledgements

My sincere thanks are due to all those people who have helped me by providing books, maps and advice. For granting access to interesting sites and allowing photographs to be taken, I would like to thank in particular Mr and Mrs Santo of Lantyan Farm, Mr B V Cock of Goodern, and the lord of the manor of Castle-by-Lantyan. I am grateful to Rev R Redrup, his son Peter and Mr Donald Curtis for some interesting information about the Tristan legend in St Kea parish. I would also like to acknowledge the help that I have received from the County Record Office and the Cornish Studies library at Redruth. I would like also to thank Alison Poole for her editing skills and Ray Bishop for his evocative photographs.

Bibliography

Béroul, The Romance of Tristan, Penguin 1985; Ditmas, E.M.R., Tristan and Iseult in Cornwall 1969; Ewart, Prof. A, The Romance of Tristan by Béroul, Vol 1. Blackwell 1939; Padel, Oliver, The Cornish background to the Tristan stories. Cambridge Medieval Celtic Studies Summer 1981. Thomas, Charles, Exploration of a drowned landscape, Batsford 1985.

Other Bossiney titles include . . .

AROUND ST AUSTELL BAY
by Joy Wilson
An exploration in words and old photographs around one of the most beautiful bays in Britain.
'. . . Joy Wilson's text is as warm and as sympathetic as the lovely old pictures, making this a book which glows with interest, a soft lamplight shedding illumination on an era dimmed by the passing years. It is a beautiful achievement . . .'
The Western Morning News

EAST CORNWALL IN THE OLD DAYS
by Joy Wilson
". . . a rich choice of early Cornish photographs . . . Joy Wilson provides an interesting starting point for the reader wanting to enjoy a journey into the past."
The Cornish Guardian

100 YEARS AROUND THE LIZARD
by Jean Stubbs
A beautiful title, relating to a magical region of Cornwall, well illustrated, with text by the distinguished novelist living near Helston.
'. . . the true flavour of life on the windswept peninsula, past and present . . . the strange qualities of the flat landscape, the effects of the elements on people's daily lives and, above all, the contrast of past and present are distilled in the text.'
Cornish Life

SEA STORIES OF CORNWALL
by Ken Duxbury, 48 photographs
'This is a tapestry of true tales', writes the author, 'by no means all of them disasters – which portray something of the spirit, the humour, the tragedy, and the enchantment, that is the lot of we who know the sea.'
'. . . a good mixture of stories, well told by a man with a close affinity to the sea and ships.'
Geoffrey Underwood, Western Evening Herald

WESTCOUNTRY MYSTERIES
introduced by Colin Wilson
A team of authors probe mysterious happenings in Somerset, Devon and Cornwall. Drawings and photographs all add to the mysterious content.
'A team of authors have joined forces to re-examine and probe various yarns from the puzzling to the tragic.'
James Belsey, Bristol Evening Post

We shall be pleased to send you our catalogue giving full details of our growing list of titles for Devon, Cornwall, Somerset, Dorset and Wiltshire as well as our forthcoming publications. If you have difficulty in obtaining our titles, write direct to Bossiney Books, Land's End, St Teath, Bodmin, Cornwall.